MEN ABOUT MEN

A GUIDE FOR WOMEN & MEN

Edited by
Wayne Meisel
and
John P. Beilenson

Designed by
SCHARR DESIGN

PETER PAUPER PRESS, INC.
WHITE PLAINS · NEW YORK

For K. P. Weseloh and Larry Beilenson

Copyright © 1992
Peter Pauper Press, Inc.
202 Mamaroneck Avenue
White Plains, NY 10601
All rights reserved
ISBN 0-88088-427-4
Printed in Hong Kong
7   6   5   4   3   2   1

Contents

Introduction

What do men think about sex, love, marriage, family and work? Just as men have asked since time immemorial, "What do women want?", women want to know "What do men think?" To find out, we've culled the words of men as ancient as Diogenes and as current as Robert Bly.

Today, men are changing. Traditional ideas about a man's role in relationships, in his family, and in the workplace are no longer adequate. Much of this flux can be attributed to the sometimes gentle and sometimes angry prodding of women during the last 20 years. Many men have listened—and often agreed—as women have challenged their aggression and emotional numbness, and their need for suffocating dominance in the bedroom and boardroom. In response, some of us have begun to reap the rewards from exploring our feelings and developing more equal relationships with women.

This process, not surprisingly, has often been confusing for men. Even as we try to remake ourselves into more sensitive, compassionate, and emotionally intimate human beings, society still feeds us images of traditional men—rugged, silent, independent, dominant—as attractive role models. This confusion provided the impetus for *Men About Men*. We thought that if we could examine the words used to describe men in the past, we might better understand our present.

As the public debate around Clarence Thomas' office behavior, William Kennedy Smith's one-night womanizing, and Mike Tyson's rape has indicated, there is considerable disagreement about what is acceptable male behavior. In each of these cases, a man's learned attitudes toward women caused emotional anguish and even physical pain. This book has provided us with a chance to check the sources of these and other beliefs.

We also wanted the opportunity to look at these issues from a masculine perspective. For many years, men have reacted to women's criticisms, either adapting or, as in these public cases, ignoring them. Now it seems time that men speak honestly about what it feels like to be a man, and raise concerns of our own. We hope that *Men About Men* can be part of this ongoing dialogue, a chance for us all to end up in a better place.

During the course of our research, we have discovered witty, stereotypical comments on men, as well as more complex and surprising observations. Many of the latter have to do with the often unexpressed pain men suffer. We've begun to question why men live ten years less than women, why they are three times more likely to commit suicide, and nine times more likely to be homeless or to be arrested for drug or alcohol violations. We may still hold the economic power in this country, but we are paying a price.

This book is meant neither to bash men nor to defend their behavior. We have merely tried to capture the heartwarming, hilarious and hateful voices that have shaped our perspective and understanding of the world. Many statements are not pleasant or happy, sensitive or just. But they do reflect the voices that we have heard over the years, voices that have helped shape our character, our actions, our values, and our definition of manhood.

The quotations in this book will, we hope, give you an understanding of what boys grow up with and what men live with. Many of the things men say and do are not acceptable. By looking at them with a clear eye, however, women and men alike can gain some understanding of where we have been and what we are up against. By examining what has been said in the past, we can use the present to re-examine, rebuild, and move forward.

J. B. and W. M.

Love

While men and women may wrangle about sex, communication, commitment and a whole range of interpersonal issues, we all want love. And men in particular—even the rugged Marlboro man when confronted with the Marlboro woman or whatever his heart secretly desires—will fall in love, sometimes quickly, often tossing reason and proportion into the nearest canyon. In literature, Romeo climbed walls and hatched elaborate plots to pursue his beloved Juliet. Tristan overcame obstacle after obstacle in order to win the fair Isolde. For love, we will do just about anything.

Things don't always work out, of course, leaving the overheated lover feeling foolish, perhaps even unmanly. Hence, there is a body of quotes that warn men away from romance, that take a more cynical view of the endeavor. But even cynics often have trouble heeding their own aphorisms. H. L. Mencken, a sarcastic observer of male-female relations, once said, "To be in love is merely to be in a state of perceptual anesthesia."

When he found the right woman later in life, however, Mencken succumbed to love's numbing charms and got married.

ᔐᔐᔐᔐᔐᔐᔐᔐᔐᔐ

Love conquers all.

VIRGIL

Venus favors the bold.

OVID

If the heart of a man is depressed with
    cares,
The mist is dispelled when a woman
    appears.

JOHN GAY,
The Beggar's Opera

No man flatters the woman he truly loves.

TUCKERMAN

It is as absurd to say that a man can't love
one woman all the time as it is to say that a
violinist needs several violins to play the
same piece of music.

HONORÉ DE BALZAC

A man falls in love through his eyes, a
woman through her ears.

WOODROW WYATT

Nobody will ever win the battle of the sexes.
There's too much fraternizing with the
enemy.

HENRY A. KISSINGER

Even the wisest men make fools of
themselves about women, and even the most
foolish women are wise about men.

THEODOR REIK

11

We love women in proportion to their degree of strangeness to us.

CHARLES BAUDELAIRE

The difference between sex and love is that sex relieves tension and love causes it.

WOODY ALLEN

Many a man has fallen in love with a girl in a light so dim he would not have chosen a suit by it.

MAURICE CHEVALIER

Love is an ocean of emotions entirely surrounded by expenses.

LORD DEWAR

Man can start with aversion and end with love; but if he begins with love and comes round to aversion he will never get back to love.

HONORÉ DE BALZAC

Love is not the dying moan of a distant violin—it's the triumphant twang of a bedspring.

S. J. PERELMAN

Men always say, "The woman *I* select." I say *they* select us. I give myself no credit for selecting.

HENRY MILLER

There are two things a real man likes— danger and play; and he likes woman because she is the most dangerous of playthings.

FRIEDRICH NIETZSCHE

Kissing don't last: cookery do.

GEORGE MEREDITH

Love is only a dirty trick played on us to achieve the continuation of the species.

SOMERSET MAUGHAM

To write a good love-letter, you ought to begin without knowing what you mean to say, and to finish without knowing what you have written.

JEAN-JACQUES ROUSSEAU

Love is the delightful interval between meeting a beautiful girl and discovering that she looks like a haddock.

JOHN BARRYMORE

14

Disguise our bondage as we will,
'Tis woman, woman, rules us still.

THOMAS MOORE

Once love is purged of vanity, it resembles a
feeble convalescent, hardly able to drag itself
about.

NICOLAS CHAMFORT

Love is an ideal thing, marriage a real thing;
a confusion of the real with the ideal never
goes unpunished.

GOETHE

Don't let love interfere with your appetite. It
never does with mine.

TROLLOPE

Marriage

After savoring the following quotes about marriage, the reader will probably come away with the notion that many men take a dim view of the institution. Besides, as a wit once quipped, "Who wants to live in an institution?" The answer, surprisingly, is men. Consider the following facts from a 1991 *Glamour* Magazine survey of statistics on men:

- Most men like being married.
- 60% say their marriage is more important than their job, friends, or other family ties.
- Men are more likely than women to want to stay in their marriage.
- While nearly 80% of divorced men, given the chance, would remarry their wives, women weren't as likely to agree.

So what's the deal? Why do guys tease others about their "ball and chain?" Why are married men supposedly "hooked" or "caught" by their women? We have several theories.

First, men may be reluctant to give up the independent, man-on-the-frontier mentality many of us take into our early 20's. This romantic notion is part of what helps define us as young men. Marriage, and its younger sibling commitment, represent the death blows to this ethos and must be challenged at each turn—until we can come to terms with a new self-image that allows us to see ourselves as members of the community, husbands and fathers in good standing.

Our second, rather Freudian, theory has to do with men's fear of women. As young children, our mothers represent God, truth, beauty—all that is good. At a certain age, however, we must turn to our fathers, learn about the hard realities of the world, and loosen the ties to our mothers. Still, we yearn for that state of absolute dependence and goodness we once knew and look for it in our romantic relationships. If we are mature enough as men, this yearning can be mediated. If not, the women in our lives may hold a tremendous amount of power to deny or grant us access to the comfort we seek. Thus, to immunize ourselves against this power, we degrade intimacy, commitment and marriage—while secretly hoping for it all along.

So much for our theories. For better or worse, we present Men on Marriage.

꒛꒛꒛꒛꒛꒛꒛꒛꒛꒛

I grunt, she fumes—it's bliss.

ROGER ROSENBLATT

Love seems the swiftest, but it is the slowest of all growths. No man or woman really knows what perfect love is until they have been married a quarter of a century.

MARK TWAIN

The long course of marriage is a long event of perpetual change, in which a man and a woman mutually build up their souls and make themselves whole. It is like rivers flowing on, through new country, always unknown.

D. H. LAWRENCE

Heaven will be no heaven to me if I do not meet my wife there.

ANDREW JACKSON

Marriage is a mistake every man should make.

GEORGE JESSEL

When a match has equal partners, then I fear not.

AESCHYLUS

By all means marry; if you get a good wife, you'll become happy; if you get a bad one, you'll become a philosopher.

SOCRATES

It is a woman's business to get married as soon as possible, and a man's to keep unmarried as long as he can.

GEORGE BERNARD SHAW,
Man and Superman

That common cold of the male psyche, fear of commitment.

RICHARD SCHICKEL

Wives are young men's mistresses, companions for middle age, and old men's nurses.

FRANCIS BACON

Bachelor's fare: bread and cheese and kisses.

JONATHAN SWIFT

To a bachelor, anyone's marriage threatens to break up the act. It's more fun being single with someone else who's also flying solo.

GERALD NACHMAN

By persistently remaining single a man converts himself into a permanent public temptation.

OSCAR WILDE

No man is regular in his attendance at the House of Commons until he is married.

BENJAMIN DISRAELI

Marriage is three parts love and seven parts forgiveness of sins.

LANGDON MITCHELL

The chain of wedlock is so heavy that it takes two to carry it—sometimes three.

ALEXANDRE DUMAS

The only thing that holds a marriage together is the husband being big enough to step back and see where the wife is wrong.

ARCHIE BUNKER

No man, examining his marriage intelligently, can fail to observe that it is compounded, at least in part, of slavery, and that he is the slave.

H. L. MENCKEN

Many a man in love with a dimple makes the mistake of marrying the whole girl.

STEPHEN LEACOCK

A man should be taller, older, heavier, uglier, and hoarser than his wife.

EDGAR WATSON HOWE

The reason why so many marriages are unhappy is because young ladies spend their time in making nets, not in making cages.

JONATHAN SWIFT

Behind every successful man you'll find a woman who has nothing to wear.

HAROLD GOFFIN

The honeymoon is over when he phones that he'll be late for supper—and she has already left a note that it's in the refrigerator.

BILL LAWRENCE

I began as a passion and ended as a habit,
like all husbands.

GEORGE BERNARD SHAW

Marriage is like a besieged fortress. Everyone
outside wants to get in, and everyone inside
wants to get out.

QUITARD

I've sometimes thought of marrying—and
then I've thought again.

NOEL COWARD

When a woman marries again it is because
she detested her first husband. When a man
marries again, it is because he adored his
first wife. Women try their luck; men risk
theirs.

OSCAR WILDE

From my experience, not one in twenty marries the first love; we build statues of snow, and weep to see them melt.

WALTER SCOTT

Most men flirt with the women they would not marry, and marry the women who would not flirt with them.

ANONYMOUS

The husband who wants a happy marriage should learn to keep his mouth shut and his checkbook open.

GROUCHO MARX

When [a man] says, "Tell me about your ex-boyfriends," he means: "Tell me about the losers and creeps." . . . When he says, "Let's talk about it some other time," he means: "The subject is closed."

BOB BERKOWITZ

You study one another for 3 weeks, you love each other 3 months, you fight for 3 years, you tolerate the situation for 30.

ANDRE DE MISSAN

American women expect to find in their husbands a perfection that English women only hope to find in their butlers.

SOMERSET MAUGHAM

Wives are people who feel they don't dance enough.

GROUCHO MARX

I have a wife, you have a wife, we all have wives, we've had a taste of paradise, we know what it means to be married.

SHOLEM ALEICHEM

Sex

Men may have ambivalent feelings about love and marriage, but they definitely enjoy sex. A man may not like to talk about his emotions, but he's happy to show his partner how he feels. Sex is physical, it's basic, and it's at least partly instinctual. And though a man's role today may be unclear at the office and at home, he seems to know how to "act like a man" in bed. (What women think of his act is the subject of another book altogether.)

Of course, men and women—especially unmarried men and women— may confuse what all this wonderful sex is about. Stereotypically, women see sex as the confirmation of love, an expression of commitment. Men often see sex as a step toward love, or simply as just plain sex. Eventually though, men and women enjoy sex for much the same reasons. A recent survey noted that the two things men liked most about sex were physical closeness and full-body embracing. Physical intimacy helps us practice for emotional intimacy. And, as we all know, practice makes perfect.

It is not enough to conquer; one must know how to seduce.

VOLTAIRE

I've looked at a lot of women with lust. I've committed adultery in my heart many times.

JIMMY CARTER

Men play the game; women know the score.

ROGER WODDIS

If it is not erotic, it is not interesting.

FERNANDO ARRABAL

Men want the same things that women want.
Men want to be loved, touched and
respected, the same as women. We should
appreciate these common threads between
us, not just get caught up in all the conflict.

MERLE ROSS

Men do make passes at girls who wear
glasses—but it all depends on their frames.

OPTICIAN

Flirtation—Attention without intention.

MAX O'NEIL

I don't like to admit it, but if a girl baited
her trap with sex, she'd catch me every
time—and it's unlikely this will ever cease to
work.

WILLIE NELSON

"Make love to every woman you meet," my uncle advised me. "If you get five percent on your outlay, it's a good investment."

ARNOLD BENNETT

Any young man who is unmarried at the age of twenty-one is a menace to the community.

BRIGHAM YOUNG

The more potent a man becomes in the bedroom, the more potent he is in business.

DR. DAVID REUBEN

Abstinence makes the heart grow fonder.

KNOX BURGER

When confronted with two evils, a man will always choose the prettier.

UNKNOWN

To succeed with the opposite sex, tell her you're impotent. She can't wait to disprove it.

CARY GRANT,
at age 72

It's stupid to be jealous of your partner's past. That's none of your business. I know Lisa had sex before we met. I can handle that. Of course she didn't enjoy it.

RICK REYNOLDS

It's okay to laugh in the bedroom so long as you don't point.

WILL DURST

The big difference between sex for money
and sex for free is that sex for money usually
costs a lot less.

BRENDAN FRANCIS

I suspect that one of the reasons we create
fiction is to make sex exciting.

GORE VIDAL

What men desire is a virgin who is a whore.

EDWARD DAHLBERG

The true feeling of sex is that of a deep
intimacy, but above all of a deep complicity.

JAMES DICKEY

A man is as good as he has to be, and a
woman as bad as she dares.

ELBERT HUBBARD

Male sexual response is far brisker and more
automatic. It is triggered easily by things—
like putting a quarter in a vending machine.

ALEX COMFORT

I tell the women that the face is my
experience and the hands are my soul—
anything to get those panties down.

CHARLES BUKOWSKI

Blondes have more fun because they're
easier to find in the dark.

UNKNOWN

Young men in contemporary culture
conclude quickly that their sexual instinct is
troublesome, intrusive, weird, and hostile to
spirit.

ROBERT BLY

Sex—the poor man's polo.
attributed to CLIFFORD ODETS

A man may sometimes be forgiven the kiss
to which he is not entitled, but never the kiss
he has not the initiative to claim.

ANONYMOUS

Most females will forgive a liberty rather
than a slight.

CHARLES C. COLTON

What men call gallantry, and gods
   adultery,
Is much more common where the climate's
   sultry.

LORD BYRON

Being with a woman all night never hurt no
professional baseball player. It's staying up
all night looking for a woman that does him
in.

CASEY STENGEL

I tend to believe that cricket is the greatest
thing God ever created on earth . . . certainly
greater than sex, although sex isn't too bad
either.

HAROLD PINTER

If you aren't going all the way, why go at all?

JOE NAMATH

Back View of 512

Family and Kids

Men tend to talk a good game when it comes to taking care of the kids, but Super Dads are as rare as four-leaf clovers. Nine out of ten men think that a father's role in raising a child is just as important as the mother's. Still, a woman generally does the bulk of the child-rearing, as well as the chores around the house—whether she works or not.

While men may not actually take care of their children, they certainly do care. Men have strong feelings about their sons and daughters, their own fathers and mothers, as well as the in-laws. Here are a few examples.

꺼꺼꺼꺼꺼꺼꺼

The most important thing a father can do for his children is to love their mother.

THEODORE M. HESBURGH

When a father, absent during the day,
returns home at six, his children receive only
his temperament and not his teaching.

ROBERT BLY

A father is a banker provided by nature.

FRENCH PROVERB

You don't have to deserve your mother's
love. You have to deserve your father's.

ROBERT FROST

One father is more than a hundred school-
masters.

ENGLISH PROVERB

Don't take up a man's time talking about the smartness of your children; he wants to talk to you about the smartness of his.

E. W. HOWE

A Jewish man with parents alive is a 15-year-old boy.

PHILIP ROTH,
Portnoy's Complaint

The father is always a Republican toward his son, and his mother's always a Democrat.

ROBERT FROST

Men are what their mothers made them.

RALPH WALDO EMERSON

What the mother sings to the cradle goes all the way down to the coffin.

HENRY WARD BEECHER

Even a secret agent can't lie to a Jewish mother.

PETER MALKIN

[Kids are] a tremendous boon to your life. If you don't do a goddamn thing but stand there and look at your kid, it takes you up, way up. Look, having a baby is very big. You don't want to make people envious or anything, but it overwhelms. Everything else is peanuts.

JACK NICHOLSON

I took a long, hard look at whether I really wanted to have children. It's beyond words what he means to me. I have everything I ever wanted in life.

ANDY MILL

Men are generally more careful of the breed of their horses and dogs than of their children.

WILLIAM PENN

Children have more need of models than of critics.

JOSEPH JOUBERT

Diogenes struck the father when the son swore.

ROBERT BURTON

Children are the wisdom of the nation.

WEST AFRICAN SAYING

The family is a court of justice which never shuts down for night or day.

MALCOLM DE CHAZAL

A child is nature's only bona fide, guaranteed positive surprise, which is why it gets hard to get it up for work.

JACK NICHOLSON

Home life as we understand it is no more natural to us than a cage is natural to a cockatoo.

GEORGE BERNARD SHAW

I don't know who my grandfather was; I am much more concerned to know what his grandson will be.

ABRAHAM LINCOLN

The first half of our lives is ruined by our parents and the second half by our children.

CLARENCE DARROW

The child is father of the man.

WILLIAM WORDSWORTH

Work and Play

Work—what we do when we leave our homes each morning—is for many of us men the defining factor in our lives. Much of our self-esteem—whatever the roles we play as husbands and fathers—derives from our jobs and the status, power and prestige we find at work. And when the 9 to 5 workday produces drudgery and disappointment, we take refuge in our leisure, and especially in our sports. Many women express frustration at men's devotion to football, baseball, basketball, hockey or whatever competition that happens to flicker across the television. But we men find some measure of peace and, as some of the quotes reveal, meaning in these "meaningless" diversions.

༺༺༺༺༺༺༺༺

Labor is man's greatest function. He is nothing, he can do nothing, he can achieve nothing, he can fulfill nothing, without working.

ORVILLE DEWEY

As a man thinks, so does he become. Every man is the son of his own works.

CERVANTES

That which does not kill me makes me stronger.

FRIEDRICH NIETZSCHE

Men are taught that their role in life is to be the bread-winner. While women are certainly members in good standing of the work-a-day chain gang, men feel that their earning power is the central factor of their existence.

BOB BERKOWITZ

My father taught me to work; he did not teach me to love it.

ABRAHAM LINCOLN

Power is what men seek, and any group that gets it will abuse it. It is the same old story.

LINCOLN STEFFENS

My young men shall never farm. Men who work the soil cannot dream, and wisdom comes to us in dreams.

WOWOKA,
*Member of a non-agricultural
tribe in Nevada*

Never underestimate a man who over-estimates himself.

FRANKLIN D. ROOSEVELT,
on General Douglas MacArthur

The real character of a man is found out by his amusements.

JOSHUA REYNOLDS

A man is rich in proportion to the things he can afford to let alone.

HENRY DAVID THOREAU

I don't drink; I don't like it—it makes me feel good.

OSCAR LEVANT

For many young men and boys, hunting is a rite of passage. When a father takes his son out hunting for the first time, there is a ritual going on that is rooted deeply in our past. . . . Dad is reliving his youth and that long-ago first day in the woods with his father, and the son is receiving a gift of time and experience that takes him a step closer to adulthood.

BOB BERKOWITZ

The best thing emerging from sports, games, work rules, winning, and losing is fairness. Not necessarily honesty—fairness.

WARREN FARRELL

You gotta be a man to play baseball for a living but you gotta have a lot of little boy in you, too.

ROY CAMPANELLA

I am convinced that every boy, in his heart, would rather steal second base than an automobile.

THOMAS CAMBELL CLARK

Nice guys finish last.

LEO DUROCHER

The right man is the one that seizes the moment.

GOETHE

Identity

During the last 20 years, as women have redefined sexual and gender roles, men have, often grudgingly, been forced to reconsider what it means to be a man. We have had our own inadequacies—our isolation, our emotional numbness, our insecurities—thrown up in our face. Not surprisingly, a few of the wittiest quotes here are self-deprecating.

One supposes that it's about time, considering our need for dominance, and our wars and violence-mongering both abroad and in our own homes. A more equitable and compassionate arrangement between the sexes is surely in order.

But what is that order? If men are not rewarded for their ability to kill and conquer, and if women can perform in the workplace as well as men, what can a man do that affirms his sense of masculinity. These are the issues that men face today. They are difficult and painful—so if your husband, boyfriend, father, brother or friend

seems to be working on them, grant him
some consideration. Unless you support
him, he is unlikely to keep trying.

゠゠゠゠゠゠゠゠゠゠

Real men don't eat quiche.

BRUCE FEIRSTEIN

Real men eat anything.

THE EDITORS

You never know till you try to reach them
how accessible men are; but you must
approach each man by the right door.

HENRY WARD BEECHER

Self-sufficiency is built into masculinity.

WARREN FARRELL

Be skilled in speech so that you will succeed.
The tongue of a man is his sword and
effective speech is stronger than all fighting.
ANCIENT EGYPTIAN WISDOM

Men may not get all they pay for in this
world, but they must certainly pay for all
they get.
FREDERICK DOUGLASS

In our civilization, men are afraid that they
will not be men enough and women are
afraid that they might be considered only
women.
THEODOR REIK

The male in the past twenty years has
become more thoughtful, more gentle. But
by this process he has not become more
free. He's a nice boy who now not only
pleases his mother but also the young
woman he is living with.
ROBERT BLY

Men growing up are rewarded socially for
eating a lot.

RYAN CASEY

Man—a creature made at the end of the
week's work when God was tired.

MARK TWAIN

Greater eaters of meat are in general more
cruel and ferocious than other men.

JEAN-JACQUES ROUSSEAU

Men wish to be saved from the mischiefs of
their vices, but not from their vices.

RALPH WALDO EMERSON

There ain't no man can avoid being born average. But there ain't no reason a man got to be common.

SATCHEL PAIGE

To me, old age is always fifteen years older than I am.

BERNARD BARUCH

Clothes make the man.

LATIN PROVERB

In our youth, one of the principal lessons imparted by our mothers was that as young, maturing Black men, we had to be "strong" at all costs. Many of our fathers reinforced this message, tempering it with the misconception that it is somehow not masculine for a "man" to have a sensitive side.

Ebony Male Magazine

There appears to be a conscience in mankind which severely punishes the man who does not somehow and at some time, at whatever cost to his pride, cease to defend and assert himself, and instead confess himself fallible and human. Until he can do this, an impenetrable wall shuts him out from the living experience of feeling himself a man among men.

FRANCIS WELLER

We are essentially little boys trapped in men's bodies. Men have to get in touch with their wealth of emotions, because, man, you could stay locked up for years. I think those are the things that kill us.

EMILIO ESTEVEZ

The survival of our society may rest on the degree to which we are able to teach men to cherish life.

COOPER THOMPSON

Why . . . do practically all men never let the women in their lives hold the remote-control gadget for the television set? *We* want to flip the TV channels, not because we're interested in knowing what's on, but because we like the feeling of changing channels as fast as we can. There is just something enormously satisfying about things that turn on, that hum, that move at our bidding.

SKIP HOLLANDSWORTH

The autonomous male, the independent, strong achiever who can be counted on to be always in control is still essentially the preferred male image.

HERB GOLDBERG

We have men among us, like the whites, who pretend to know the right path, but will not consent to show it without pay! I have no faith in their paths, but believe that every man must make his own path!

BLACK HAWK,
Sauk

Friendship is held to be the severest test of character. It is easy, we think, to be loyal to family and clan, whose blood is in our own veins. Love between man and woman is founded on the mating instinct and is not free from desire and self-seeking. But to have a friend, and to be true under any and all trials, is the mark of a man!

CHARLES ALEXANDER EASTMAN,
Santee Sioux

I wished to be a brave man as much as a white boy desires to be a great lawyer or even president of the United States.

CHARLES ALEXANDER EASTMAN

We have a difficult time in this culture appreciating the wounds that a man carries. For the most part, men's wounds remain invisible, guarded by sentinels of denial, heroism, and isolation. The lessons began early and the teachings were clear: Do not expose your pain, for if you do you will be seen as weak and a failure.

FRANCIS WELLER

A man who hates dogs and loves whiskey can't be all bad.

W. C. FIELDS

Throughout the literature of feminism, there runs a puzzled complaint: Why can't men *be* men, and just relax? The reason is that, unlike femininity, relaxed masculinity is at bottom empty, a limp nullity. While the female body is full of internal potentiality, the male is internally barren. Manhood at the most basic level can be validated and expressed only in action.

GEORGE GILDER

We must learn to live together as brothers or perish together as fools.

MARTIN LUTHER KING

61

Boys will be boys, and so will a lot of
middle-aged men.

KIN HUBBARD

Old men love to give advice to console
themselves for not being able to set a bad
example.

LA ROCHEFOUCAULD

What's a man's age? He must hurry more,
   that's all;
Cram in a day what his youth took a year
   to hold.

ROBERT BROWNING

He that falls in love with himself will have no
rivals.

BENJAMIN FRANKLIN

I sometimes think that God, in creating man, somewhat overestimated his ability.

OSCAR WILDE

To say that a man is made up of certain chemical elements is a satisfactory description only for those who intend to use him as a fertilizer.

HERBERT J. MULLER

A man who won't die for something is not fit to live.

MARTIN LUTHER KING, JR.

Since I've left my father's house at age 18, I've only lived with one man—and that's me.

ROBIN MACNEIL